How to create a cult-like following

The fastest way to build a cult-like following happens to also be the simplest.

Everyone has a natural tenancy to want to believe in something greater than themselves, all you need to do is give them a reason.

INTRODUCTION

Individuals want to have confidence in some-thing, become the point of convergence of such want by offering them or cause, another confidence to pursue.

Keep your words ambiguous yet brimming with promise and exact excitement over level-headedness and consistent judgment, give your new supporters customs to perform(rituals), request that they make relinquishes for the greater good, under no circumstance can you let them know that in fact, this will be for your benefit. By having a religion-like setting and excellent causes, your new framework will bring you untold power.

You will be surprised just how far your followers will go for you when they truly believe in either your cause or you as a person, this can lead you to almost any desire. POWER AND WEALTH, HONOUR AND PRIDE, AUTHORITY AND POWER, perhaps revenge is your goal or something that transcends all of them. whatever you desire can be made easier with a cult-like following that is well built and thoroughly managed.

The investigation of a con artist or how to make a loyal following in five simple stages.

In looking as you should for the techniques that will give you the most influence with the least struggle you will discover that the making of a faction that is cult-like is amongst the best. Having a huge following afterall opens up a wide range of potential outcomes for misdirection not exclusively will your supporters adore you they will guard you against your foes and will wilfully help you by alluring others to join your enticing group. This sort of intensity will lift you to another domain, you will never again need to battle or utilise deception to authorise your will, you are revered and can't be blamed under any circumstance, you may believe it's an enormous undertaking to make such a following however in certainty it is genuinely straightforward.

As individuals we have an urgent need to have faith in something, anything, this makes us naive, we just can't endure extensive durations of uncertainty that comes from a scarcity of belief, you need to dangle some new cause, solution, get wealthy fast system or the most recent technological trend and the people will leap from the water in order to join you.

This is verified in history the records of the new trends and cults that have created a mass following for themselves might fill a library, and

after the greatest of times have passed they typ-
ically look ridiculous however at the time they
made they were not only engaging but maybe
some even reached a level that can be
called nothing less than therefore transcenden-
tal therefore divine.

Always in a rush to believe in one thing or another we'll makers saints and faiths out of nothing or out of something we don't even under-
stand, don't let the naivety of people go to
waste present yourself as the article of worship,
create folk to cult around you.

The great cult makers of the sixteenth and seventeenth centuries have mastered the art of cult-creating, they lived in somewhat similar times to us, a time that organised faith was on the decline and science on the increasing rise, we would rally round the new cause or religion. The cult makers begun by presenting health elixir and shortcuts to wealth, moving quickly from city to city they originally targeted on little groups and out of the blue they stumble on the reality of human nature, the larger the group you get around yourself the easier it is to convince them of an ideal, if you only speak to a few people, sure some might join but if get yourself in front of thousands and millions of people than the chances to grow your following is increased tenfold.

there is no better time to implement this I mean if you don't have a social presence on the internet can you even be called relevant?

When people say all you need to do is put yourself out there they are on the right track as this is essentially the first step.

Speak with Passion and enthusiasm that way any problems that arise will be met with a violent reaction, anyone who dares to sow a seed of doubt against your belief, consciously learning this dynamic over time and experimenting in sudden unforeseen situations cult makers formed the science of captivating and holding a crown, moulding the group into followers and therefore the Followers into a cult.

This may seem like that is no longer applicable in this day and age but you would be dead wrong,

the best organisations on the planet are masters
of making a cult-like following.

let me give you some examples, Apples mar-
keting strategies masterfully made so that they
are devoted even if you disagree with this what
other explanation can you come up with that
their following is willing to spend hundreds
of pounds more on a device that gets outper-
formed and is cheaper than theirs.

How do you explain the standing in line for well over 8 hours just to buy an overpriced device?

Apple has absolutely mastered the art of building a cult-like following there are many more examples where we can find organisations like this, they are in business, fashion, politics, art, they may not even know how they achieved their result but you can be far more deliberate in your workings of the growth.

Simply follow the five stages of cult-building that our ancestors formed over the years.

STAGE 1

Keep your plan obscure with simplicity.

To create a devoted following you need to get people interested first, do not try to do this with blatant actions that are too clear and straightforward however through words that are ambiguous and deceptive.

Your initials speeches, conversations, and dis-cussions should comprise of two main compo-nents.

On the one hand the encouragement of some-thing exceptional and transformative.

On the other a mist of complete vagueness.

This combination will arouse every kind of hazy fantasies in your listeners who will cre-ate their own associations and see what they need to visualise, as a result of its unclearness your charm ought to even be apparent, most people's concerns have advanced causes, interconnected social factors that are that can be tracked back in your past and are extremely arduous to unravel, nevertheless you must have the endurance to take care slowly, the general public craves to listen to an easy answer that can cure their issues. The power to supply this type of resolution can provide you with power while building your following.

STAGE 2

Emphasise the visual and the feeling over the intellectual.

Once groups have begun to assemble around you two main dangers will manifest them-selves.

Boredom and disbelief.

Boredom can make the groups of people go else-where and disbelief can give them the space to think logically about whatever it is that you're offering them, squandering away the cloud you have got skilfully constructed and revealing your ideas for what they are.

You need to amuse the board then keep at bay the skeptics, the most effective method to do this is thru theatre or alternative devices of its kind,

surround yourself with lavishness this will hypnotise your followers with visual lustre, fill their eyes with spectacle, not solely can this

keep them from seeing the faults of your i-
deas, and the gaps in your belief system, it'll
bring a lot of attention and eventually a
lot of followers, charm all their senses, use
fragrance for scent, soothing music for hear-
ing, vibrant diagrams and graphs for the eye-
s. You may even stimulate the mind maybe
by some new technological devices or other
devices, as long as you do this they won't be
thinking deeply about the actual meaning of
what you are doing, use the exotic remote cul-
tural strange customs to make theatrical effects
and to create the foremost common and stand-
ard matters seen as something extraordinary.

STAGE3

Borrow the structure of organised religion to construct your following.

Your cult-like following is expanding, it's time to organise it.

Find a way, both elevating and encouraging.

Organised religions have long commanded undoubted authority for enormous amounts of individuals.

Create ceremonies for your followers to follow, organised into a hierarchy, ranking them in ranks of virtue and giving them names and titles that resound with spiritual suggestions, ask of them to make sacrifices that may increase your treasury and if you this money smartly increase your power.

Not always does increased money also increase your power and authority but it sure helps.

Emphasise your gatherings as something sacred, you must act as a sort of prophet, you're not a dictator. You're a priest, a guru, a sage, or the other word that hides your real power within the haze of religion.

this stage is extremely important because this is where their loyalties will be tested and the followers that preserver past here will prove to be devoted, this cannot be rushed take your time to convince them don't be rash but you must also be dynamic in your movements so not to let potential followers slip away.

STAGE 4

Disguise the source of your financial gain.

Your organisation has expanded considerably by this point and you have organised it into a church-like form. Your income is also increasing thru your follower's donations and sacrifices, you must under no circumstance be seen as greedy for cash and consequently the power it brings. After all your true goal is not to gain power and money, these are the simply consequences that come from having a devoted following.

It is at this time that you should disguise the source of your financial gain, your followers need to believe that if they follow you all kinds of advantages will fall on them. By encompassing yourself with luxury you become a living testimony of the soundness of your belief system. don't ever acknowledge that your wealth and success really comes from your follower's, instead make it appear that it comes from your methods and lifestyle.

The only situation where you would openly reveal the fact that you have far more to gain from this partnership than they do is if you have a plan already in place to deal with this, whatever it may be.

Followers will try to replicate your every move with the hope to reach the level of success and luxury you have shown them and there are eagerness and enthusiasm will delude them of any misleading nature of your financial gain.

STAGE 5

There must always be an enemy

The final stage is more about being able to grow and maintain your following and for that to happen you must have an enemy or naysayers for no revolution or great movement has ever succeeded without some sort of conflict and resistance.

And if you don't have any direct opposition make one!!!

Your following is now massive and a thriving magnet attracting a lot more followers, you no longer need perform grand speeches or explain your belief system, for the most part, because your devoted followers now do this for you, they are the living testimony, and are willing to speak on your behalf.

However, If you're not careful laziness can set in along with boredom and can demagnetise the following, even if it does not affect the most devoted followers it can be a slippery slope if you let this happen for too long so keep your following engaged with new ideas and always seem ahead of the game, like the fashion industry does as well and any tech industries always trying to be the first to release the new gadget or fashion trend.

To maintain your followers united you need to do what all religions and belief systems or great industries have done and Create an Enemy dynamic.

First, ensure your follower's belief is strong by

making them believe that when you join you they are part of an exclusive club or a grand movement united by a bond of common goals than to strengthen this bond construct the notion of an insidious enemy intent on bringing you and your flock to ruin,"There is be a unit of non-believers that will do anything to stop" that way any outsider who tries to reveal any misleading in your belief system can be delineated as a member of this insidious unit.

If you have got no enemies, invent one!!!! Giving your followers something to react against they will tighten and unite even further, after all, they have your cause to believe in and any unbelievers are either not welcome or ready for conversion.